Schaum
Making Music Method
Level Three

By John W. Schaum
Revised and Edited by Wesley Schaum

FOREWORD

This edition of the Schaum *Making Music Method* is the product of many years of teaching experience and continuing evaluation. Many careful refinements include revised explanations and instructions that highlight the learning points as they are presented.

Note reading proficiency is promoted by showing the student how to recognize various patterns in the melody, accompaniment and rhythms, indicated by phrase marks.

Metronome marks indicate the ***lowest to highest range*** within a tempo. The lowest markings are the minimum tempo acceptable for performance. Faster tempo markings are for students with more ability and for those who prefer the faster tempo as a matter of personal taste. Striving for the faster tempo is also a good incentive for the student to practice more.

Measure numbers in a small box are included at the beginning of each system of music. This makes it easier to locate measures during the lesson and for written practice assignments. The first *complete* measure is considered measure number 1.

Self-help is encouraged by the inclusion of ***Reference Pages*** and a ***Music Dictionary***.

Much of music is *original*, composed by John W. Schaum. There are also transcriptions of folk songs and themes from various American and European composers.

The Schaum *Making Music Method* consists of ***eight books***, from Primer Level through Level 7.

NOTE TO PARENTS

Regular practice is essential for progress at the piano. Assist your child by setting a consistent time for practice each day (except weekends and holidays). If practice is missed on a weekday, it could be made up during the weekend.

Quality of practice is more important than quantity. Try to plan household events to avoid interruptions and distractions during practice time. When practice is careful and attentive, 20 to 30 minutes per day is sufficient at this level.

Schaum Publications, Inc.
10235 N. Port Washington Rd. • Mequon, WI 53092
www.schaumpiano.net

01-34
AQ-32

2

CONTENTS

Schaum's Curriculum for Musicianship Development

Student musicianship is developed by a balanced curriculum that includes:
- Note Reading and Music Theory
- Finger Strength and Dexterity
- Rhythmic Training and Ensemble Experience
- Music Appreciation and Repertoire Development

These practical supplementary books help to achieve musicianship goals:

Theory
Arpeggio Speller
Rhythm Workbook, Level 3
Scale Speller
Theory Workbook, Level 3

Technic
Around the World In All Keys
Fingerpower, Level 3
Masters of Technic, Level 3

Note Reading
Sight Reading Workbook, Level 3

Music Appreciation and Repertoire
Christmas Solos, Level 3
Easy Master Themes, Level 3
Folk Song Solos, Level 3
Jazz Styles, Level 3
Patriotic Solos, Level 3
Sacred Solos, Level 3

All books are published and copyrighted by Schaum Publications, Inc. – www.schaumpiano.net

First and Second Endings.

The signs: [1.] [2.] mean that when you repeat the piece (play it the second time), do not play the measure marked **1,** but play the measure marked **2** instead.

Change of Dynamics with Repeat Signs.

The dynamic mark, *p-f* in measure 1 means to play *p* through the 1st ending. When repeating, play *f* through the 2nd ending.

Surfside Serenade

Allegro ♩ = 116-138

Italian Folk Song

p-f Come, down to the sea, Surf -

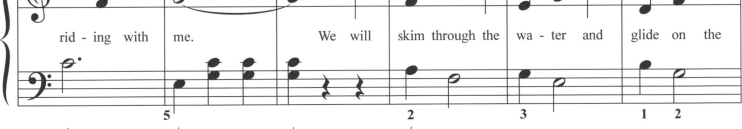

rid - ing with me. We will skim through the wa - ter and glide on the

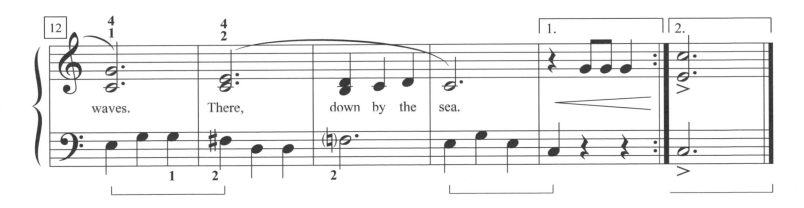

waves. There, down by the sea.

4

Accent Marks

Accent marks are placed above or below a note. Accented notes should be played with extra stress or emphasis, somewhat louder than notes without accents.

The loudness of an accent depends on the dynamic mark in use. For example, a small accent in a measure marked *f* will be louder than a small accent in a measure marked *p*.

These are three common accent marks:

— = small accent   > = medium accent   ∧ = big accent

*Farandole

Presto ♩= 184-208

*Georges Bizet (1838-1875)

*Georges Bizet (bee-ZAY) Great French composer of opera. This piece uses a theme from his opera "L'Arlesienne."
A *farandole* is an old folk dance from southern France accompanied by flute and drum, often performed on holidays.

Schaum Flash Cards – Root Position Triads

These flash cards contain various white key triads, from which broken chords are derived and found in many of the pieces that follow.

The flash cards are designed to be used as a unit in this book or used individually (cut apart on the dotted lines). *Answers* are printed on the back side to make it easter to use at the lesson or at home.

At first, work on groups of four triads each week, one line at a time. As the student becomes more proficient, additional triad groups may be added.

Recommendations for use:

• Play and name the letter names of the notes, from the bottom up.

• Play and name the *root* (bottom note) by saying the letter name.

• Play and name the *third* (middle note) by saying the letter name.

• Flash cards should be *reviewed* frequently.

• May also be *used at home* with help from parents

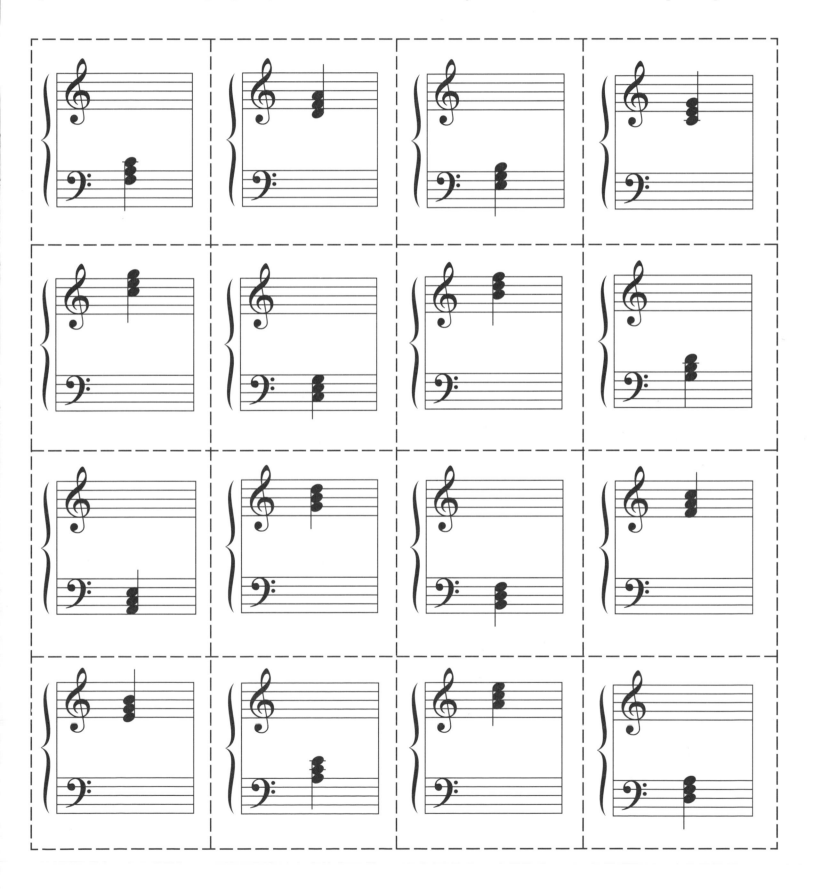

The answers are printed on the back of each flash card for the convenience of parents and teacher

Treble Clef	Bass Clef	Treble Clef	Bass Clef
G (Fifth)	B (Fifth)	A (Fifth)	C (Fifth)
E (Third)	G (Third)	F (Third)	A (Third)
C (Root)	E (Root)	D (Root)	F (Root)

Bass Clef	Treble Clef	Bass Clef	Treble Clef
D (Fifth)	F (Fifth)	G (Fifth)	G (Fifth)
B (Third)	D (Third)	E (Third)	E (Third)
G (Root)	B (Root)	C (Root)	C (Root)

Treble Clef	Bass Clef	Treble Clef	Bass Clef
C (Fifth)	F (Fifth)	D (Fifth)	E (Fifth)
A (Third)	D (Third)	B (Third)	C (Third)
F (Root)	B (Root)	G (Root)	A (Root)

Bass Clef	Treble Clef	Bass Clef	Treble Clef
A (Fifth)	E (Fifth)	E (Fifth)	B (Fifth)
F (Third)	C (Third)	C (Third)	G (Third)
D (Root)	A (Root)	A (Root)	E (Root)

Glass Bottom Boat

Moderato ♩ = 100-116

Notice *f* for the left hand melody and *p* for the right hand accompaniment.

Teacher's Note. ***Independence of the hands*** can be developed by optional ***cross-hands*** practice. Play the treble clef part of this piece with the *left* hand and the bass clef part with the *right* hand. The fingering would have to be revised. Other pieces in this book on pages 4, 30 and 42 may also be played in cross-hands style.

8

Finger Workout
Play this exercise five times daily as a warm-up for "Circus Capers."

Círcus Capers

Vivace ♩ = 152–184

The left hand accompaniment pattern is the *same in every measure*, throughout the piece. Play it one octave lower than written.

(Play one octave lower than written.)

Musical Form. This piece has two sections – **A** and **B**. It begins with section **A** (measures 1-8). Then section **A** is repeated (measures 9-16). Section **B** is next (measures 17-24). Then section **A** is repeated once more (measures 25-32). Therefore the musical form is **A-A-B-A**. Knowing the form will make learning and memorizing easier.

For more information see page 32.

10

Importance of Phrase Marks.

Observing phrase marks will help make reading and learning music easier. In the bass staff, notice that the left hand accompaniment has *two patterns that are repeated throughout the piece*. Each pattern is indicated with a phrase mark.

The melody in the treble staff also has phrases that are repeated. For example, the two phrases in the first line of music are repeated in the 3rd line of music. Likewise, the first two phrases in the 2nd line of music are used again in the 4th line.

Song of the Gondolier

Allegretto ♩. = 60-72

*Emile Paladilhe (1844-1926)

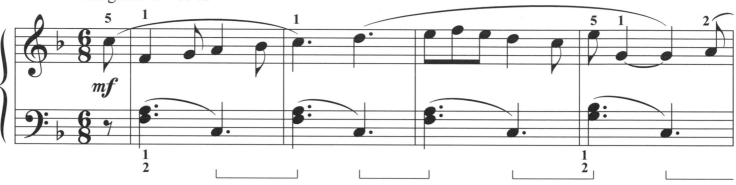

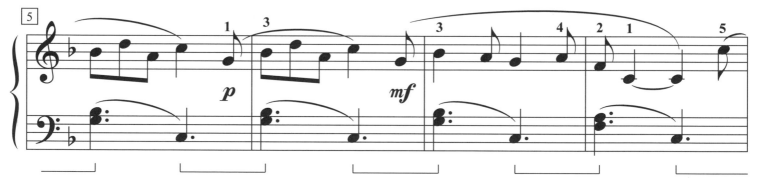

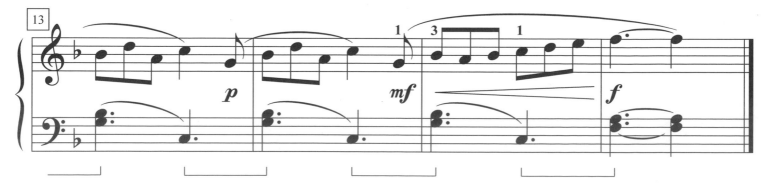

* Emile Paladilhe (pah-lah-DEEL) was a French composer who wrote music in an Italian style.

Triplet. A triplet is a group of three notes of equal value. The three notes of a triplet fit into the *same time span as two regular notes* of the same value. In this piece, the three notes of the 8th note triplet fit into one beat.

Triplets are usually marked by an italic (slanted) number 3 and a bracket. The bracket may be curved or straight, as shown here:

Fireworks

Stephen Heller (1813-1888)

Spiritoso ♩ = 92-112

Teacher's Note: The counting of triplet groups is purposely left to the preference of the teacher. Saying a three syllable word such as "trip-oh-let," "beau-ti-ful" or "choc-o-late" often helps the student to feel the rhythm. Setting a metronome to click on each note of a triplet or on the *first note* of each triplet may also be helpful.

Legato Pedal. The inverted v-shaped pedal mark shown in the sample is called *legato pedal* or *syncopated pedal*. The toe makes a quick up-and-down movement at the same time as the note is played on the first beat of each measure. This allows one measure to blend smoothly into another, thus the name legato pedal.

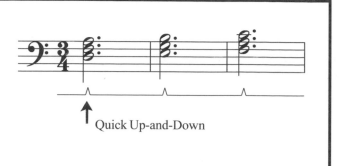

↑ Quick Up-and-Down

Be careful – the pedal must come *UP at exactly the same time as the hands play the notes* on the first beat. The pedal is IMMEDIATELY LOWERED to make the sound more *legato* (smooth and connected). The quick up-and-down foot movement resembles a "hiccup."

Pedal Study   Directions: Learn to play the notes and correct rhythm first. Next, play the entire study using left hand and pedal. Then play both hands with pedal. Use a much slower metronome speed when first adding the pedal.

Pedal Waltz

This waltz is based on the *Pedal Study* above. Follow the same directions as for the *Pedal Study*.

The legato pedal is commonly used to *avoid blurring* of one note or chord into another. Pedal changes may occur with *any note* and on *any beat* in a measure.

Notice that in this piece, many measures have pedal changes on the 1st and 3rd beats.

Cookout

Look for left hand broken chord patterns that recur in the accompaniment.

Allegro ♩ = 104-120

*Allan Macbeth (1856-1910)

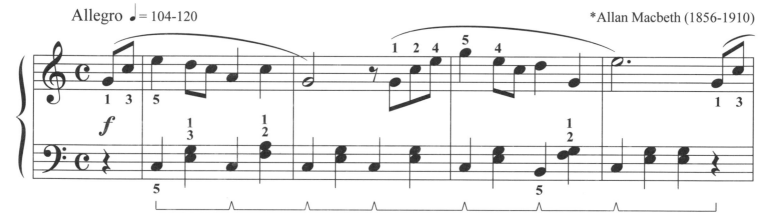

* Allan Macbeth, Scottish composer, conductor, choirmaster and organist in several Glasgow churches.

14

Finger Patterns.

Notice that the right hand *fingering is the same* in almost every measure throughout the piece. Also look for left hand *patterns that are repeated* in the accompaniment on both pages. This will help you to read the notes and make playing this piece easier.

The notes for both hands in measures 1 through 13 are *repeated* in measures 17 through 29.

The sign *15ma* (sometimes 16) means to play the notes *two octaves higher* than written.

8va means to play the notes *one octave higher*.

Whirlwind

Allegretto ♩ = 112-138

*Stephen A. Emery (1841-1891)

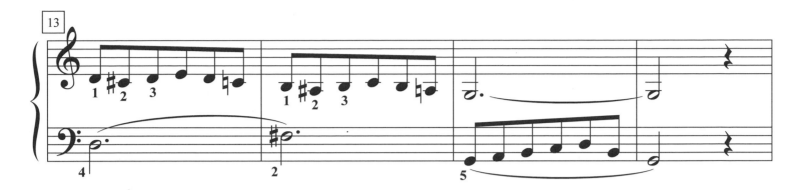

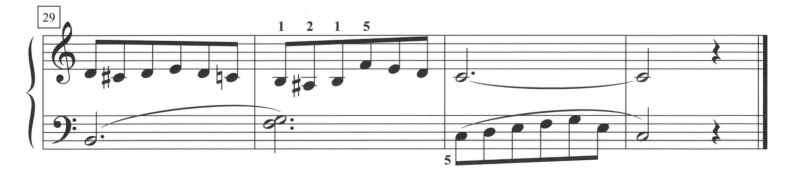

*Stephen A. Emery was an American composer born in Maine. He became a teacher at the New England Conservatory and at Boston University. His compositions include piano pieces, string quartets, vocal music and music textbooks.

16

Key of E Major

Key signature has four sharps: F♯, C♯, G♯, D♯. Play this scale of E major five times daily as a warmup.

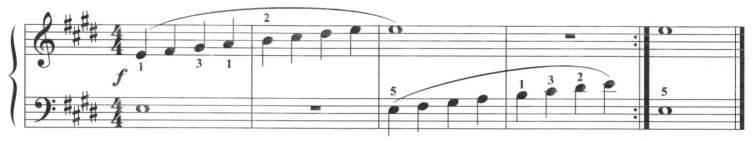

*Ship Ahoy!

Moderato ♩ = 108-120

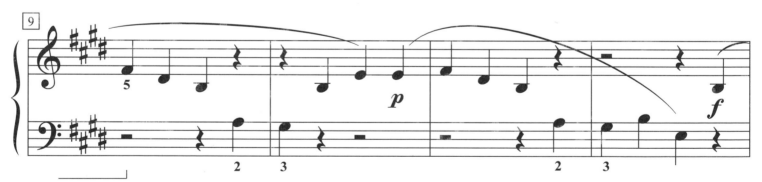

Ahoy is an expression called out by sailors to greet or get the attention of someone within shouting distance.

Cross Hand Accompaniment (Left Hand).
The first beat of the accompaniment is the note with *stem down* in the bass staff. For the 2nd and 3rd beats, the left hand crosses over the right hand and plays the notes with *stem up* in the treble staff. The left hand notes should be played softly.

The right hand plays the melody notes, which are connected with a broken line.

Blow the Man Down

Andante ♩ = 80-92

*Sea Chantey

* Look up "chantey" in the Music Dictionary on page 48.

Lincoln and Music

In the presidential election of 1860, special words were written for Lincoln's campaign song. The three states in which Lincoln lived are mentioned in the lyrics: Kentucky, Indiana (the Hoosier state) and Illinois.

Lincoln's favorite waltz, "Silver Bell," is on the next page. His favorite pianist was Louis Gottschalk (see page 45).

Lincoln's Campaign Song ("Lincoln and Liberty")

*See footnote page 19.

Allegro ♩ = 138-160

Hur-rah for the choice of the na-tion, Our chief-tan so brave and so true. We'll go for the great ref-or-ma-tion, For Lin-coln and Lib-er-ty too! We'll go for the son of Ken-tuck-y, The he-ro of

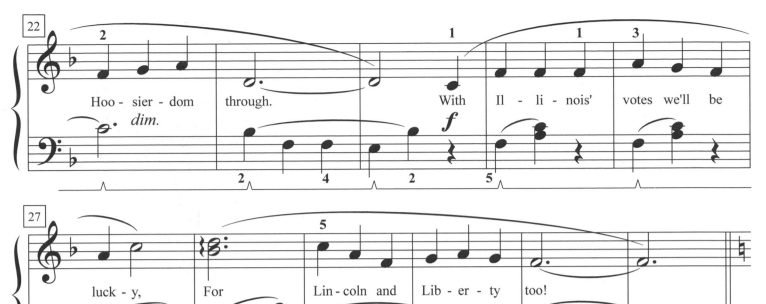

Hoo - sier - dom   through.   With   Il - li - nois'   votes we'll be

dim.

luck - y,   For   Lin - coln and   Lib - er - ty   too!

Lincoln's Favorite Waltz ("Silver Bell")

Moderato ♩ = 108-120

Rolled Chord. A wavy line to the left of an interval or chord indicates that it is to be played in arpeggio style as a rolled chord. This means the notes should be played one at a time, starting with the bottom note, rapidly moving up to the top note. The bottom note is started slightly before the beat so that the top note is played exactly on the beat. All notes are to be held so that they blend together to form the interval or chord.

Shared Beams. The beams in the first three measures have stems going up and down. Notes in the *treble staff* are to be played with the *right* hand. Notes in the *bass staff* are to be played with the *left* hand. Because all the notes share the same beam, no rests are needed.

Notice that the *notes in these measures are the same*, played one octave lower each time.

Look for left hand accompaniment patterns that recur. This makes it easier to read and memorize.

Water Ballet

A.P. Wyman

Grazioso ♩ = 88-100

℅ Espressivo ♩ = 108-120

(continue same fingering)

2nd time to Coda

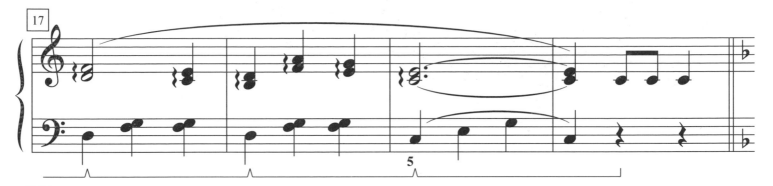

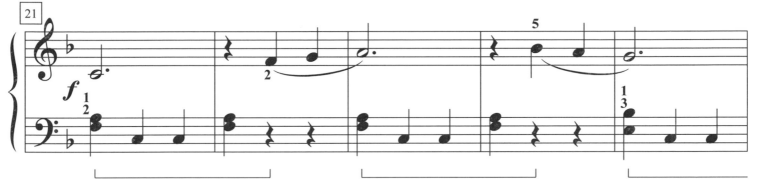

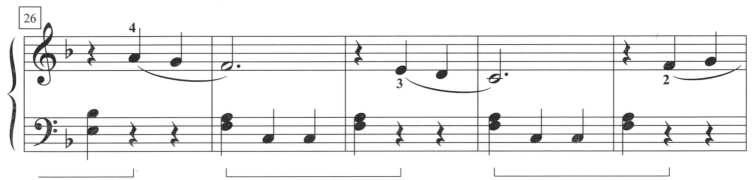

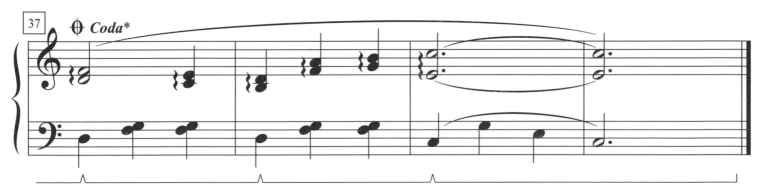

* A *coda* is a short section at the end of a piece of music.

   D.S. al coda = *dal segno* (dahl SEN-yoh) means go back to the sign 𝄋 and repeat until "2nd time to Coda."

   Then skip to the coda ⊕ and play to the end.

*School Rally

Moderato ♩ = 104-116

Allan M. Hirsh

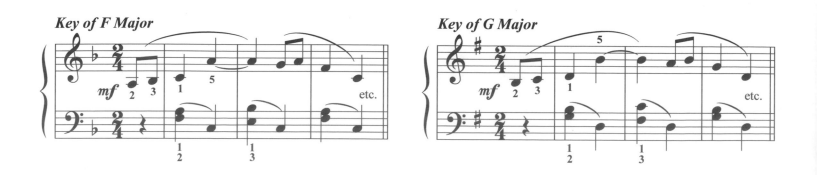

*The theme for this piece is based on "Boola, Boola," the famous football song of Yale University in New Haven, Connecticut.

Transposing (optional extra work). To transpose is to **change the key** of a piece of music. It means a different key signature and different starting notes in both hands. If desired, use separate manuscript paper to write out the piece, otherwise the piece may be worked out by ear at the keyboard. In this piece, the fingering remains the same when transposing to the two keys below. Notice that the left hand has only two accompaniment patterns.

Key of F Major

Key of G Major

Making Music Quiz No. 1

DIRECTIONS: Match each musical term in the left column with the correct definition in the right column. Write the alphabetical letter of the definition on the proper line. For example, number **1** (Vivace) means <u>lively, full of energy</u>; therefore the letter **Q** has been placed on the line. If necessary, refer to the Reference Pages (front and rear inside covers) or the Music Dictionary (page 48).

Q 1. Vivace   A. big accent

_____ 2. [music notation]   B. Lincoln's favorite waltz

_____ 3. A-A-B-A   C. short section at end of a piece

_____ 4. 15ma - - - - -   D. French composer of opera

_____ 5. [music notation: 1. 2.]   E. rolled third

_____ 6. Presto   F. "Blow the Man Down"

_____ 7. [music notation]   G. triplet

_____ 8. Allan Macbeth   H. return to the sign: 𝄋 and play to _fine_ (end)

_____ 9. [music notation]   I. very fast

_____ 10. ⊕ _Coda_   J. American composer

_____ 11. Bizet   K. change to a different key

_____ 12. 8vb - - - - -   L. legato pedal mark

_____ 13. famous sea chantey   M. first ending, second ending

_____ 14. ʌ   N. example of musical form

_____ 15. transpose   O. octave lower sign

_____ 16. Stephen Emery   P. Key of E Major

_____ 17. [music notation]   Q. lively, full of energy

_____ 18. _D.S. al fine_   R. Scottish composer

_____ 19. [music notation: triplet]   S. play two octaves higher

_____ 20. "Silver Bell"   T. triad

Teacher's Note: If desired, this quiz may be graded. Give 5 points for each correct answer.
A total score of 65 is passing – 70 is fair – 80 is good – 90 is very good – 95 or above is excellent.

Grace Note. A grace note is a very small note played quickly *before* the principal note (full size note). The principal note is played *on the beat*.

A grace note has no time value and does not affect the counting of the principal note. A grace note is affected by a key signature and previous accidentals in the same measure.

Dance Recital

Franz Schubert (1797-1828)
Op. 94, No. 3

Grazioso ♩ = 108-120

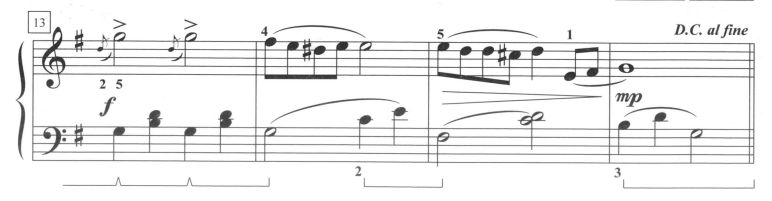

Crushed Grace Note.

The grace notes in this piece are intended to produce a percussive effect, imitating the drone bass of a Scottish bag pipe.

Here, the grace note is played *at the same time* as the principal notes. The grace note is *immediately released* while the principal notes are held.

Notice that this style of grace note is different than on page 24.

Scotland's Great Poet
Robert Burns (1759-1796) wrote these words to go with this old Scottish tune:

A Highland Lad my love was born,
  The Lowland Lads he held in scorn,
But he still was faithful to his clan
  My gallant brave John Highland man!
Sing hey, my brave John Highland man,
  Sing ho, my brave John Highland man!
There's not a lad in all the land,
  To match my brave John Highland man!

Highland Lad

Old Scottish Air

Animato ♩ = 108-126

Johannes Brahms is one of the famous *Three B's of music*: Bach, Beethoven and Brahms. All were German composers who lived at different times. Bach lived from 1685 to 1750 and Beethoven from 1770 to 1827. Their music is some of the greatest ever written.

Brahms' reputation is based mainly on his orchestral music (4 symphonies, 2 piano concertos and a violin concerto) along with numerous chamber music and piano solo compositions. He also wrote a large quantity of vocal and choral music.

Viennese Waltz

Brahms (1833-1897)
Op. 39, No. 2

Dolce ♩ = 96-108

Johann Strauss, Jr. came from a family of performers and composers. His father, Johann, Sr. is known as the "Father of the Waltz." His two brothers were also musicians. Each one was the conductor of his own dance orchestra. All were born in Austria.

Johann, Jr. is famous as the **Waltz King** because he wrote almost 500 pieces of dance music, the majority of which were waltzes. He is the composer of the "Blue Danube Waltz," probably the best known waltz ever written.

Thousand and One Nights

Grazioso ♩ = 132-152

Johann Strauss, Jr. (1825-1899)

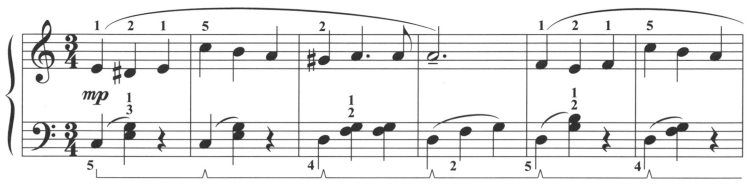

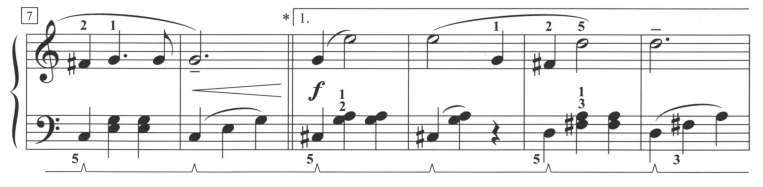

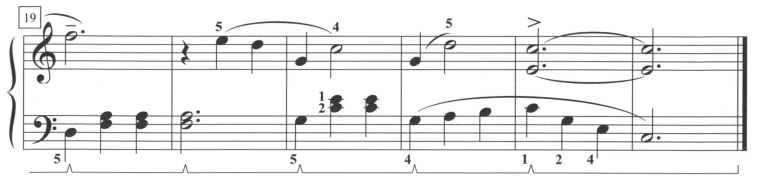

* Notice that the **1st ending** extends from measure 9 through measure 16.
The **2nd ending** begins at measure 17 and continues to the end.

28

Change of Key. The first page of this piece is in the key of *C minor*. Starting in measure 21, the key changes to *C major*. Listen for the difference in sound between the major and minor keys.

Introduction. The first four measures serve as an introduction, setting the mood for this piece. The melody starts in measure 5.

Carmencîta

Robert Vollstedt (1854-1919)
Op. 151

Vivo ♩ = 144-168

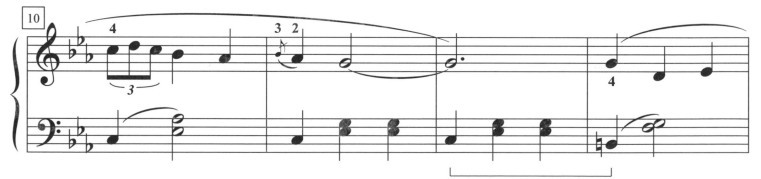

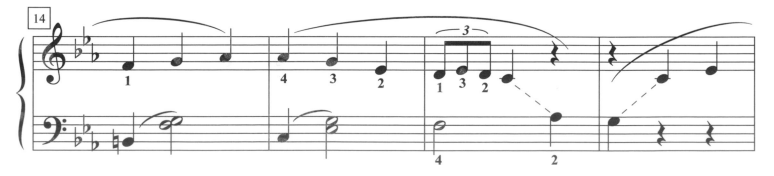

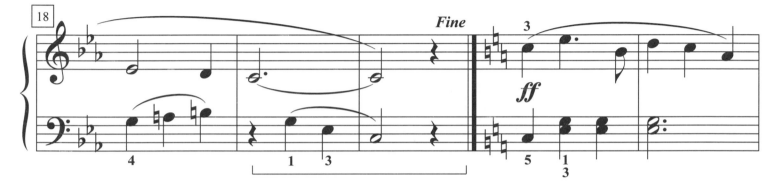

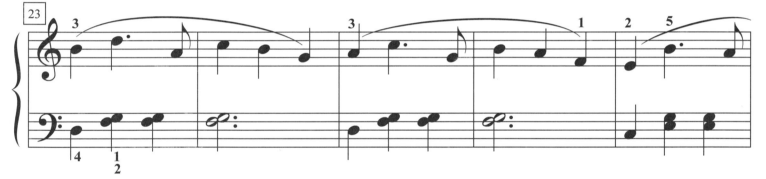

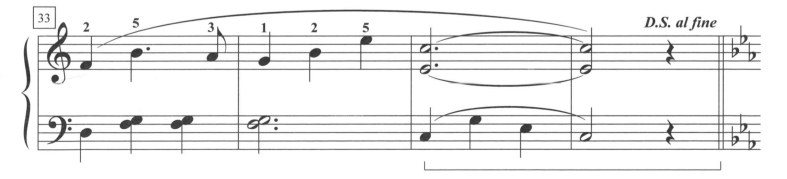

30

Key of A-flat Major. The key signature in this piece has *four flats* (from left to right): B♭, E♭, A♭ and D♭. The key gets its name from the 2nd last flat to the right.

Notice that the right hand accompaniment has only *two different intervals:*

Stage Coach

Spiritoso ♩ = 88-108   Play the right hand accompaniment *softly* throughout.

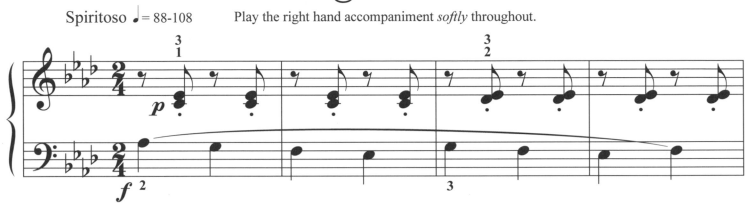

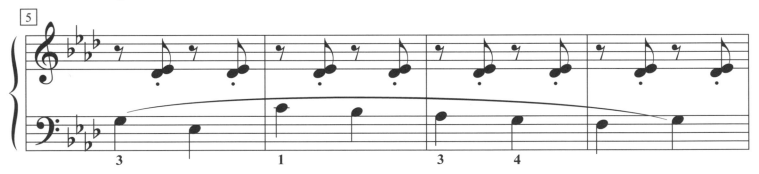

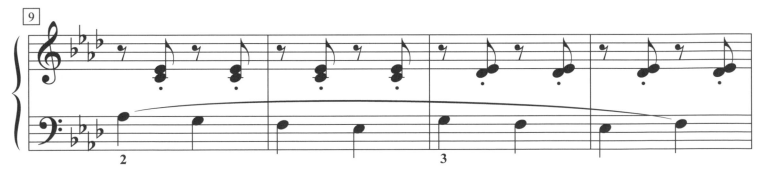

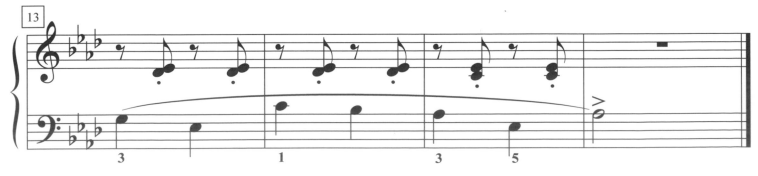

Grace Note Interpretation. The style, mood and tempo of music determines how a grace note is played. In pieces like this one, with a fast tempo or with a style that is bold or vigorous, a ***crushed*** grace note should be played (see measure 10).

In music with a moderate to slow tempo, or with a graceful style, a ***separated*** grace note should be played (see page 24).

Dance of the Clowns

*Rimsky-Korsakov (1844-1908)

*Nicholas Rimsky-Korsakov (RIM-skee CORE-sa-kov) Famous Russian composer of operas and orchestral music.

**Play *f* the first time – play *p* when repeated. See page 3.

A-A-B-A Form. Composers plan their music with an outline called a *form*. This is similar to the way an architect plans a building. This piece is organized into two sections of music labeled **A** and **B**. The beginning of each section is indicated with a *red letter* in a circle.

Section **A** is repeated two times. The first repetition of **A** begins at measure 8 with the right hand playing *one octave higher*. The second repetition of **A** begins at measure 24. Notice that the *fingering is the same* each time section **A** is repeated.

A-A-B-A form also is used in the music on pages 9 and 45. Other common musical forms are A-B-A and A-B-A-B. Look for these forms and others when reviewing or memorizing other pieces.

Baton Twirler

Animato ♩= 126-152

*George F. Root (1820-1895)

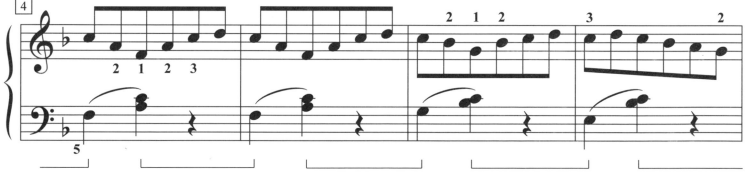

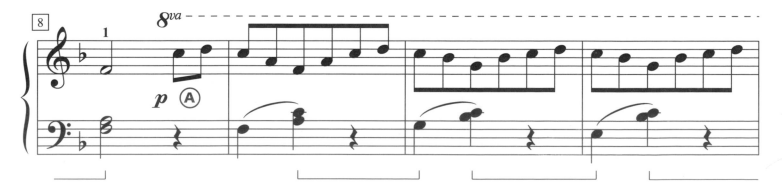

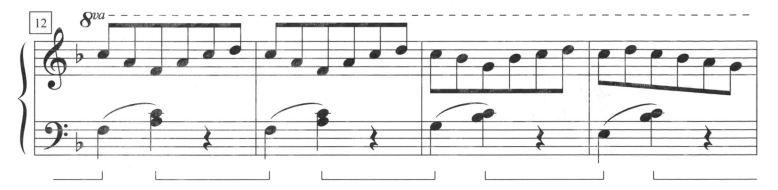

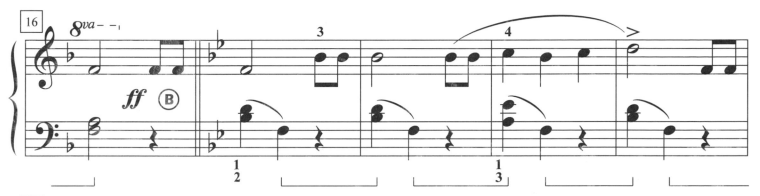

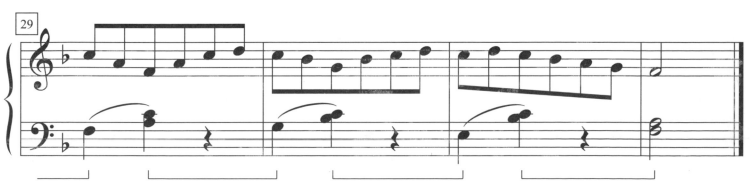

* George F. Root was an American composer born in Massachusetts. His most famous song is "Battle Cry of Freedom," written during the Civil War.

Northern Lights

Allegretto ♩ = 116-138

*Grieg (1843-1907)
Op. 12, No. 7

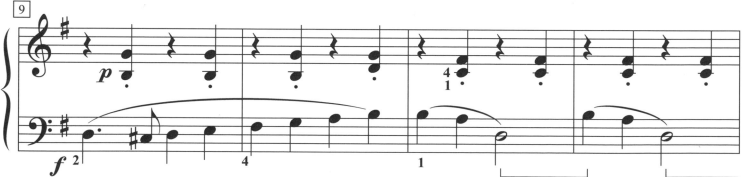

*See page 39.

Triplet Brackets.

All the 8th notes in this piece are triplets. Notice that the triplet brackets are used *only in the first two measures*. For the rest of the piece, the brackets are omitted and only a beam connects the three 8th notes of each triplet.

Cartwheels

*Schumann (1810-1856)
Op. 68, No. 14

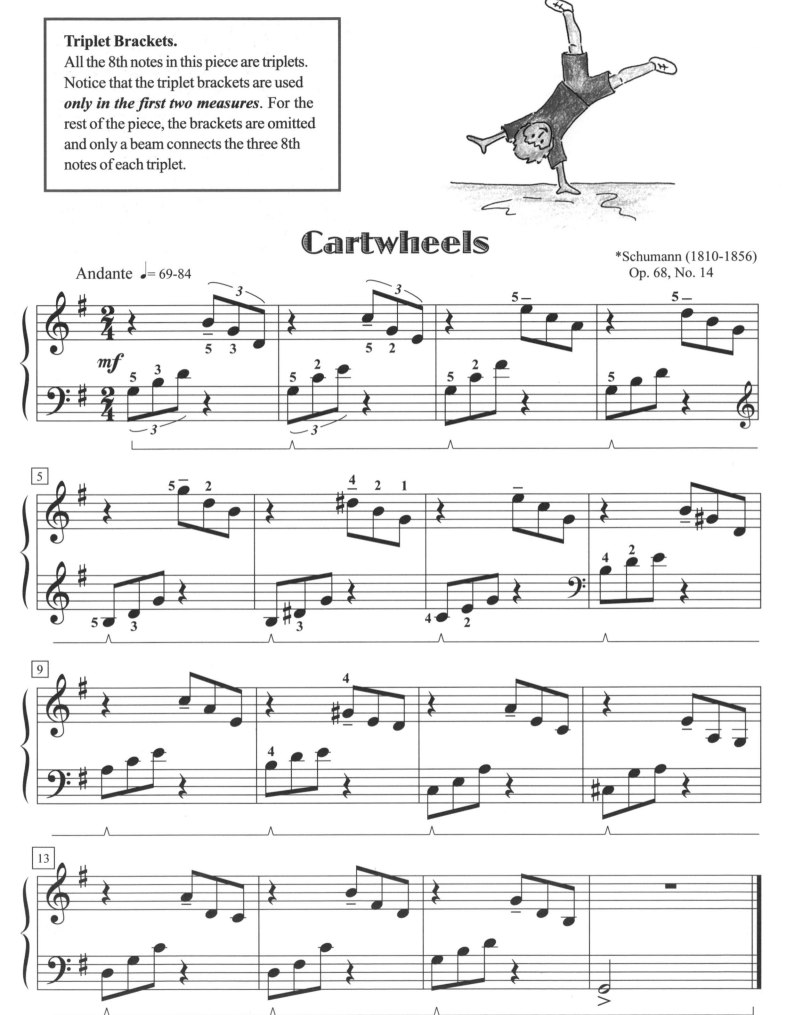

*See page 39.

Dotted 8th and 16th Note.

The dotted 8th note is usually combined with a single 16th note. When connected by a beam, the 16th note has a short double beam, as shown below. A dotted 8th and 16th together make one beat in 2/4, 3/4 and 4/4 time, the same as one quarter note. Here is a sample of the counting:

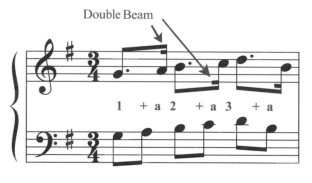

This flag is like the one that flew over Fort McHenry in Baltimore, Maryland (see footnote on page 37). Notice that the flag has only 15 stars because there were only 15 states in the United States at the time.

Star-Spangled Banner

Words by Francis Scott Key (1779-1843)

Music by John Stafford Smith (1750-1836)

The words for the "Star-Spangled Banner" were written as a poem by Francis Scott Key during the war of 1812. At the time, Key left Baltimore with a flag of truce to contact the British fleet for the purpose of releasing of a captured friend. The British would not allow Key to return for fear that their intended attack on Baltimore would be disclosed. Key was kept under protective custody and compelled to witness the bombardment of Fort McHenry. He anxiously watched the flag at the fort through the whole day. During the night he watched the bomb shells and at early dawn he saw the proudly waving flag of our country, which inspired him to write these words. Key's verses were later set to music originally titled, "To Anacreon In Heaven."

Wolfgang Amadeus Mozart (MOE-tsahrt) was born in Austria and is generally considered one of the world's greatest composers. He was a child prodigy trained by his father. By age 5, Mozart started composing his own music and by age 12 had given hundreds of recital performances throughout Europe.

Turkish March

W.A. Mozart (1756-1791)

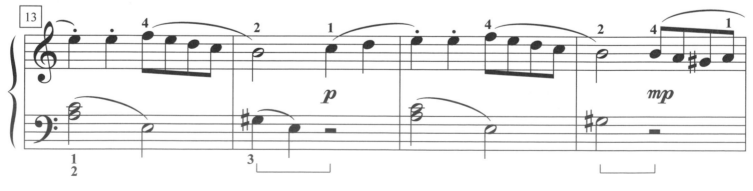

(see page 34)

Edward Grieg (GREEG) Norway's most famous composer. His best known works are his "Piano Concerto in A Minor" and the "Peer Gynt Suites" for orchestra.

(see page 35)

Robert Schumann (SHOO-man) A German composer best known for his piano works. *Cartwheels* (page 35) uses a theme from his "Album For the Young."

(see page 40)

Peter Ilyitch Tchaikowsky (chy-CUFF-skee) A famous Russian composer best known for his "Nutcracker Suite," symphonies, ballets and piano concertos. *Reflections In the Water* (page 40) is a theme from the 2nd movement of his Piano Concerto No. 1.

Change of finger on the same note.
In measure 15, the right hand fingering is **1-2**. This means that at first, play the note with your thumb. Then, while holding the note down, change to your 2nd finger.

Reflections In the Water

Semplice ♩ = 108-120

*Tchaikowsky (1840-1893)
Op. 23

*See page 39.

The Trill.

The trill is a musical ornament performed by rapidly alternating the principal note (printed note) and the note on the scale degree above. It is abbreviated by the symbol *tr* written above the principal note and followed by a wavy line.

In measures 1 and 7 of this piece, the trill notes are written as 16th notes. In other measures the trill symbol is used.

*Bird Migration

*The trills in this piece represent the bird calls of warblers and canaries. The two-note phrases portray the chirping of other birds.

Teacher's Note: The trills used here are simple measured trills, with all trill notes of equal value. The trills are played only on white keys. Other kinds of trills, including those with varying rhythm and accidentals, are presented later.

42

$\begin{matrix} 9 \\ 8 \end{matrix}$ This time signature indicates 9 beats per measure, with an 8th note getting one beat.

♪ = 1 beat   ♩ = 2 beats   ♩. = 3 beats   𝅗𝅥. = 6 beats

Weeping Willow

Cantabile ♩. = 66-76

Squirrels In the Park

44

Accompaniment Patterns.
Phrase marks in the bass staff help you find different patterns in the accompaniment. Many of these patterns are used several times.

Notice that the third line of music is almost the same as the first line, except for the accompaniment in measure 12.

Rush Hour Downtown

Vivo ♩ = 152-176

William Ganz (1833-1914)

Mardi Gras

Animato ♩ = 112-126

*Louis M. Gottschalk
(1829-1869)

*Louis M. Gottschalk was born in New Orleans, Louisiana. He was one of the first Americans to achieve fame as a concert pianist and composer. Gottschalk concertized extensively in France, Switzerland, Spain and the United States. Between 1862 and 1865 he performed 1100 concerts, an amazing number for the time.

Making Music Quiz No. 2

DIRECTIONS: Match each musical term in the left column with the correct definition in the right column. Write the alphabetical letter of the definition on the proper line. For example, number **1** (Three B's of music) is <u>Bach, Beethoven and Brahms</u>; therefore the letter **M** has been placed on the line. If necessary, refer to the Reference Pages (front and rear inside covers) or the Music Dictionary (page 48).

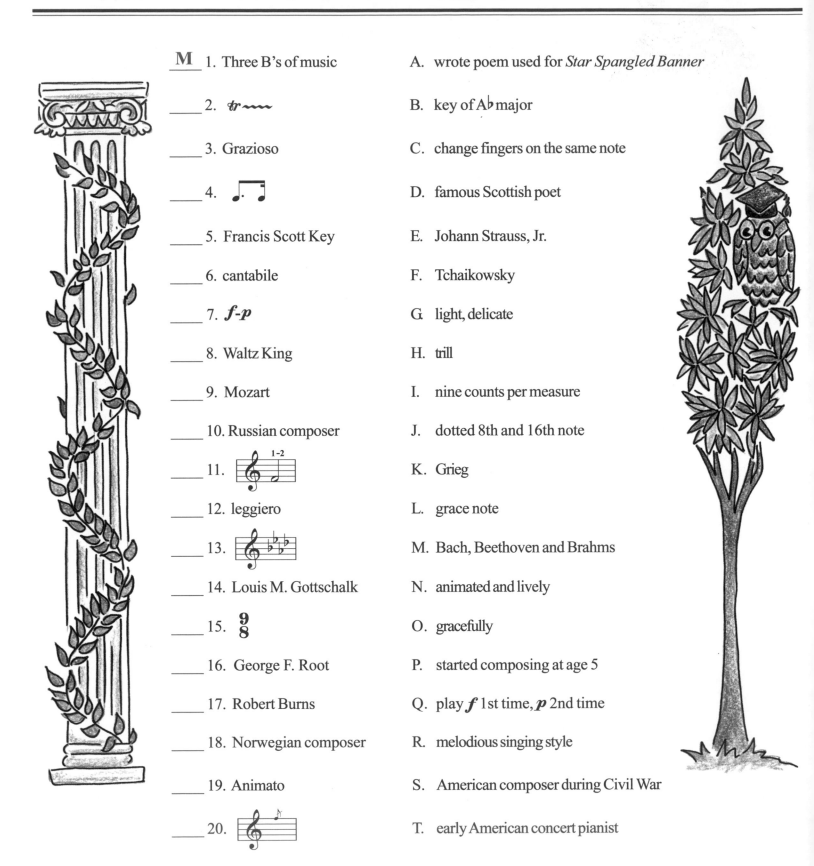

_M_ 1. Three B's of music — A. wrote poem used for *Star Spangled Banner*

_____ 2. _tr_ ~~~ — B. key of A♭ major

_____ 3. Grazioso — C. change fingers on the same note

_____ 4. — D. famous Scottish poet

_____ 5. Francis Scott Key — E. Johann Strauss, Jr.

_____ 6. cantabile — F. Tchaikowsky

_____ 7. *f-p* — G. light, delicate

_____ 8. Waltz King — H. trill

_____ 9. Mozart — I. nine counts per measure

_____ 10. Russian composer — J. dotted 8th and 16th note

_____ 11. — K. Grieg

_____ 12. leggiero — L. grace note

_____ 13. — M. Bach, Beethoven and Brahms

_____ 14. Louis M. Gottschalk — N. animated and lively

_____ 15. $\frac{9}{8}$ — O. gracefully

_____ 16. George F. Root — P. started composing at age 5

_____ 17. Robert Burns — Q. play *f* 1st time, *p* 2nd time

_____ 18. Norwegian composer — R. melodious singing style

_____ 19. Animato — S. American composer during Civil War

_____ 20. — T. early American concert pianist

Teacher's Note: If desired, this quiz may be graded. Give 5 points for each correct answer.
A total score of 65 is passing – 70 is fair – 80 is good – 90 is very good – 95 or above is excellent.

Certificate
of Progress

This certifies that

_____

has successfully completed

LEVEL THREE

of the Schaum
Making Music Method

and is eligible for advancement to
LEVEL FOUR

_____
Teacher

_____
Date

MUSIC DICTIONARY

*Also see musical signs and symbols
on front and rear inside covers.*

Terms listed here are limited to those commonly found in Level Three methods and supplements. Pronunciations have accented syllables shown in capital letters.

For a more complete listing, the *Schaum Dictionary of Musical Terms* is a separate 1500-word compilation especially for keyboard students.

accel. = **accelerando** (ahk-sell-er-ON-doh) Gradually increase the tempo while playing.

accent marks: _ > ʌ See page 4.

adagio (ah-DAH-jee-oh) Slow, slowly.

allegretto (ah-leh-GRET-toh) A little slower than *allegro*.

allegro (ah-LEH-grow) Fast, quickly.

andante (ahn-DAHN-tay) Moderately slow.

andantino (ahn-dahn-TEE-noh) A little faster than *andante*.

animato (ah-nee-MAH-toh) Lively, spirited.

arioso (ah-ree-OH-soh) Song-like, graceful, melodious.

arpeggio (are-PED-jee-oh) Playing the notes of a chord one at a time consecutively, up or down.

a tempo (ah TEHM-poh) Return to the previous tempo.

cantabile (cahn-TAH-bil-lay) Singing style.

chantey (CHAN-tee) Work song sung by sailors, often in rhythm with their work motions.

chord (KORD) Simultaneous sounding of three or more notes.

chromatic (kro-MAH-tik) Series of notes proceeding by half steps.

coda (KOH-dah) Extra musical section at the end of a piece. Often indicated by the symbol: ⊕

con brio (kone BREE-oh) With vigor, spirit, gusto.

con vivo (kone VEE-voh) With life, animated.

cresc. = **crescendo** (cre-SHEN-doh) Gradually increasing in loudness. Also abbreviated: ◁

D.C. = **da capo** (dah KAH-poh) Return to the beginning and repeat.

D.C. al fine (ahl FEE-nay) Return to the beginning and repeat, ending at the word *Fine*.

dim. = **diminuendo** (di-min-you-END-oh) Gradually playing less loudly. Also abbreviated: ▷

dolce (DOL-chay) Sweetly, softly.

D.S. = **dal segno** (dahl-SEN-yoh) Return to the sign 𝄋 and repeat.

D.S. al fine Return to the sign 𝄋 and repeat, ending at the word *Fine*.

dynamics Signs used to show different levels of loud and soft. For example, *p* *mf* *ff*

8va Abbreviation for *octave higher sign*.

8vb Abbreviation for *octave lower sign*.

energico (eh-NAIR-jee-koh) Energetic, powerful.

fermata (ferr-MAH-tah) Hold or wait on a note or chord longer than its normal duration. Symbol: ⌢

15ma Play two octaves higher than written.

fine (FEE-nay) End. (see *D.C. al fine* and *D.S. al fine*)

fz = **forzando** (fohr-TSAHN-doh) With force, energy.

giocoso (jee-oh-KOH-soh) Humorously, playfully.

grace note ♪ Musical ornament. See page 24.

grazioso (graht-zee-OH-soh) Gracefully.

hold Name sometimes given to a *fermata*: ⌢

larghetto (lahr-GET-oh) Tempo a little faster than *largo*.

largo (LAHR-goh) Very slow, solemn.

legato (lah-GAH-toh) Notes played in a smooth and connected manner. Usually indicated with a *phrase mark*.

leggiero (led-jee-AIR-oh) Light, delicate. Abbreviation: *legg.*

lento (LEN-toh) Slow, but not as slow as *largo*.

L.H. Abbreviation for left hand.

maestoso (my-ess-TOH-soh) Majestic, dignified, proudly.

meno mosso (MAY-noh MOHS-soh) Less motion, less quickly.

moderato (mah-dur-AH-toh) At a moderate tempo.

molto (MOHL-toh) Very, much.

octave (AHK-tiv) Interval of an 8th. The top and bottom notes have the same letter name.

octave signs Numbers indicating the notes to be played higher or lower than written. Often used with a dotted line above or below the notes affected. Abbreviations: *8* *8va* *8vb* *15ma*

op. = **opus** (OH-puss) Unit of musical work usually numbered in chronological order. May be a composition of any length, from a short single piece to a full symphony.

phrase mark Curved line placed over or under groups of notes, indicating the length of a phrase. The notes within a phrase are usually played *legato*.

piu mosso (PEE-oo MOHS-soh) More motion, faster.

poco a poco (POH-koh ah POH-koh) Little by little, gradually.

presto (PRESS-toh) Very fast, faster than *allegro*.

R. H. Abbreviation for right hand.

rit. = **ritardando** (ree-tahr-DAHN-doh) Gradually slow the tempo while playing.

ritard. Another abbreviation for *ritardando*.

scherzando (skare-TSAHN-doh) Playfully, jokingly.

scherzo (SKARE-tso) Light, playful or humorous piece of music. *Scherzo* literally means joke.

semplice (SEMM-plee-chay) Simple, plain.

sfz = **sforzando** (sfor-TSAHN-doh) Sudden emphasis or accent on a note or chord.

spiritoso (spir-ih-TOH-soh) Animated, with spirit.

syncopation (sink-uh-PAY-shun) Rhythmic emphasis of notes OFF the regular numbered counts.

transpose (trans-POZE) To play a melody or chord in a different key, starting on a higher or lower note. When transposing, a different key signature, notes from a different scale and a different hand position are used.

triad (TRY-add) Chord with three notes.

trill Musical ornament. Symbol: *tr*〜〜 See page 41.

triplet Group of three notes of equal value, played in the same time span as two regular notes of the same value. See page 11.

vivace (vee-VAH-chay) Lively, quick.

vivo (VEE-voh) Lively, animated.